I0811748

Nature's Classroom

WATER

IZZI HOWELL

PowerKiDS press

Published in 2025 by The Rosen Publishing Group, Inc.
2544 Clinton Street, Buffalo, NY 14224

First published in Great Britain in 2023 by Wayland
Copyright © Hodder and Stoughton Limited, 2023

All rights reserved.

No part of this book may be reproduced in any form without permission in writing from the publisher, except by a reviewer.

We recommend adult supervision at all times while doing the activities in this book. Always be aware that materials may contain allergens, so check the packaging for allergens if there is a risk of an allergic reaction. Anyone with a known allergy must avoid these. Also:

- Wear an apron and cover surfaces.
- Tie back long hair.
- Ask an adult for help with cutting.

Words in bold appear in the glossary on page 30.

Author and editor: Izzi Howell
Series designer: Rocket Design (East Anglia) Ltd
Consultant: Steve Parker

Picture acknowledgements: Amanita Silvicora, Jane Semina and Tancha cover and title page, Margaret Jone Wollman cover, vectortatu 3tl and 11b, BigMouse 3tr and 18t, CRStocker 3bl, tandaV 3br and 29b, ArtMari 4t, Magicleaf 4b, Juliasart 5t, Nadzin 5bl, Pogorelova Olga 5br, CRStocker 6t, ActiveLines 6bl, Rustic 6br, logistock and Vector_Up 7t, mhatzapa 7b, Drp8 8–9, Elegant Solution 9t, Oceloti 10-11b, mme mpl 10b, Simply Amazing and MiOli 11t, Designua 12t, yul1 illustrator 12b, Tetiana Peliustka, StockSmartStart, mapichai, Midorie and Amjad Hossain 13t, NMacTavish 13b, VectorMine 14t and 15b, Seahorse Vector 14b, wickerwood 15t, KajaNi 16, Lemberg Vector studio 17l, creatOR76 17r, Great-Stock and Flash Vector 18t, Maquiladora 18b, Kazakova Maryia 19t, Eloku 19b, SaveJungle, Kazakova Maryia, Volkonskaia Ekaterina, Vitaly Ilyasov, sozai-koyomi and BlueRingMedia 20t, BluedarkArt 20b, Spreadthesign 21t, AnnstasAg 21b, zombiu26 22-23, Studio_G 23t, Olkita 24, ryho 25t, Macrovector 25bl, elenabsl 25br, topvector 26t, ClassicVector 26b, NTL studio 27, Bubushonok and johavel 28, Ksenia_designer 29t, NotionPic 31.

All additional design elements from Shutterstock or drawn by designer.

Every effort has been made to clear copyright. Should there be any inadvertent omission, please apply to the publisher for rectification.

The website addresses (URLs) included in this book were valid at the time of going to press. However, it is possible that contents or addresses may have changed since the publication of this book. No responsibility for any such changes can be accepted by either the author or the publisher.

All facts and statistics were up to date at the time of press.

Cataloging-in-Publication Data

Names: Howell, Izzi.
Title: Water / Izzi Howell.
Description: Buffalo, New York : Powerkids Press, 2025. | Series: Nature's classroom | Includes glossary and index.
Identifiers: ISBN 9781499445701 (pbk.) | ISBN 9781499445718 (library bound) | ISBN 9781499445725 (ebook)
Subjects: LCSH: Water--Juvenile literature.
Classification: LCC GB662.3 H68 2025 | DDC 553.7--dc23

Manufactured in the United States of America

CPSIA Compliance Information: Batch #CSPK25. For further information contact Rosen Publishing at 1-800-237-9932.

Find us on

CONTENTS

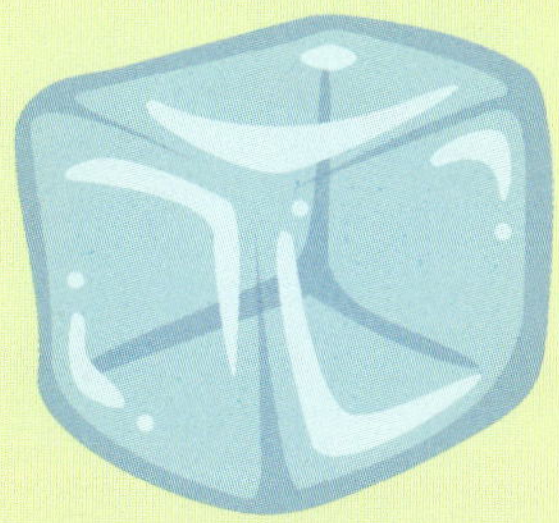

WONDERFUL WATER

There's a reason they call Earth the blue planet!

WATER EVERYWHERE

Water is found in many places on Earth, from tiny puddles to massive lakes. Rivers flow across the land and into the ocean. There is also water underground and up in Earth's **atmosphere**.

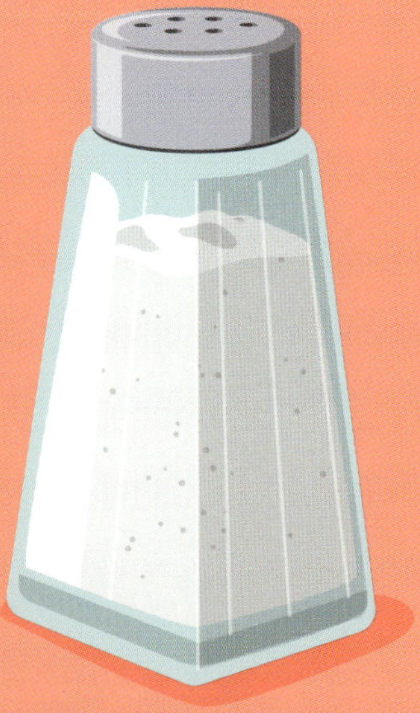

FRESH OR SALTY?

There are two main types of water: fresh water and salt water. Fresh water is found in lakes, rivers, frozen **ice caps,** and under the ground. Salt water, which is found in the seas and oceans, is too salty for us to drink.

I WONDER WOW!

MANY OCEAN ANIMALS CAN DRINK SALT WATER, INCLUDING FISH, SEA TURTLES, AND SOME SEABIRDS.

WATER FACTS

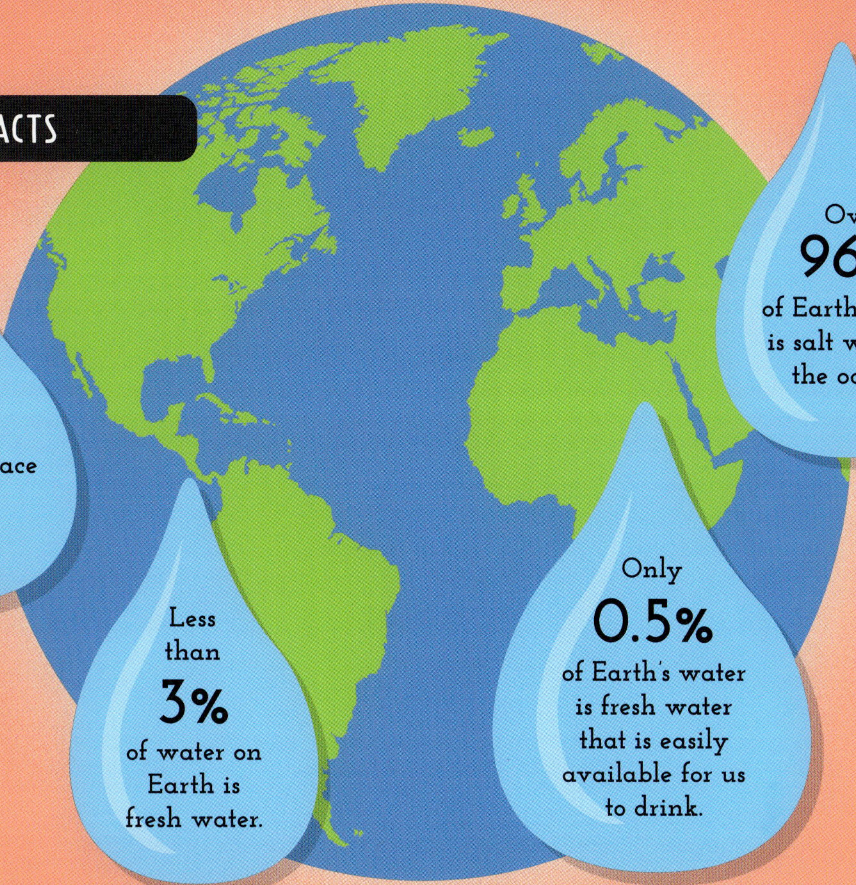

Around **71%** of Earth's surface is covered in water.

Less than **3%** of water on Earth is fresh water.

Only **0.5%** of Earth's water is fresh water that is easily available for us to drink.

Over **96%** of Earth's water is salt water in the oceans.

A DRINK AND A HOME!

Water is essential for life. All living things need to drink water—plants, animals ... and humans, of course! Water is also an important habitat for living things. Many **ecosystems** are found under and near water.

OUTDOOR OBSERVATIONS

Take a walk with an adult and see how long it takes you to spot some water in your neighborhood. It could be a big body of water like a river, or something much smaller like a pond or puddle!

SOLID, LIQUID, GAS

Water exists in three states in nature.

LIQUID STATE

We most commonly see water in its liquid state. This is because water is a liquid at temperatures between 32°F (0°C) and 212°F (100°C). Liquid water flows in lakes, rivers, and the oceans. It also falls from the sky as rain.

COLD AS ICE

In chilly places or at cold times of the year, you might see water in its solid state—ice. Liquid water freezes into ice at temperatures below 32°F (0°C). Ice, snow, frost, icicles, and hail are all types of frozen water.

LIQUID

ICE

GET OUT THERE!

TEST WATER EVAPORATION

Pour the same amount of water onto a paved surface outside on a cold, cloudy day and a warm, sunny day. Time how long it takes to disappear in each case.

QUIZ-TASTIC!

AT WHICH TEMPERATURE DOES WATER BOIL?

a) 77°F (25°C) b) 167°F (75°C) c) 212°F (100°C)

GAS? WHERE?

It's impossible to see water in its gas form because water vapor is invisible! However, we can spot **evaporation**. This is when liquid water turns into a gas. You can see the effects of evaporation when you hang wet laundry outside. The heat of the sun makes the water evaporate, which is why sunny days are best for drying laundry.

FOLLOW THAT RIVER!

Rivers flow from their source to the sea.

READY, SET, FLOW!

A river's source is the place where it starts. This is usually high in the hills or mountains. A river's source can be:

- melting ice or snow
- falling rain
- water from deep underground that has come to Earth's surface.

A RIVER'S PATH

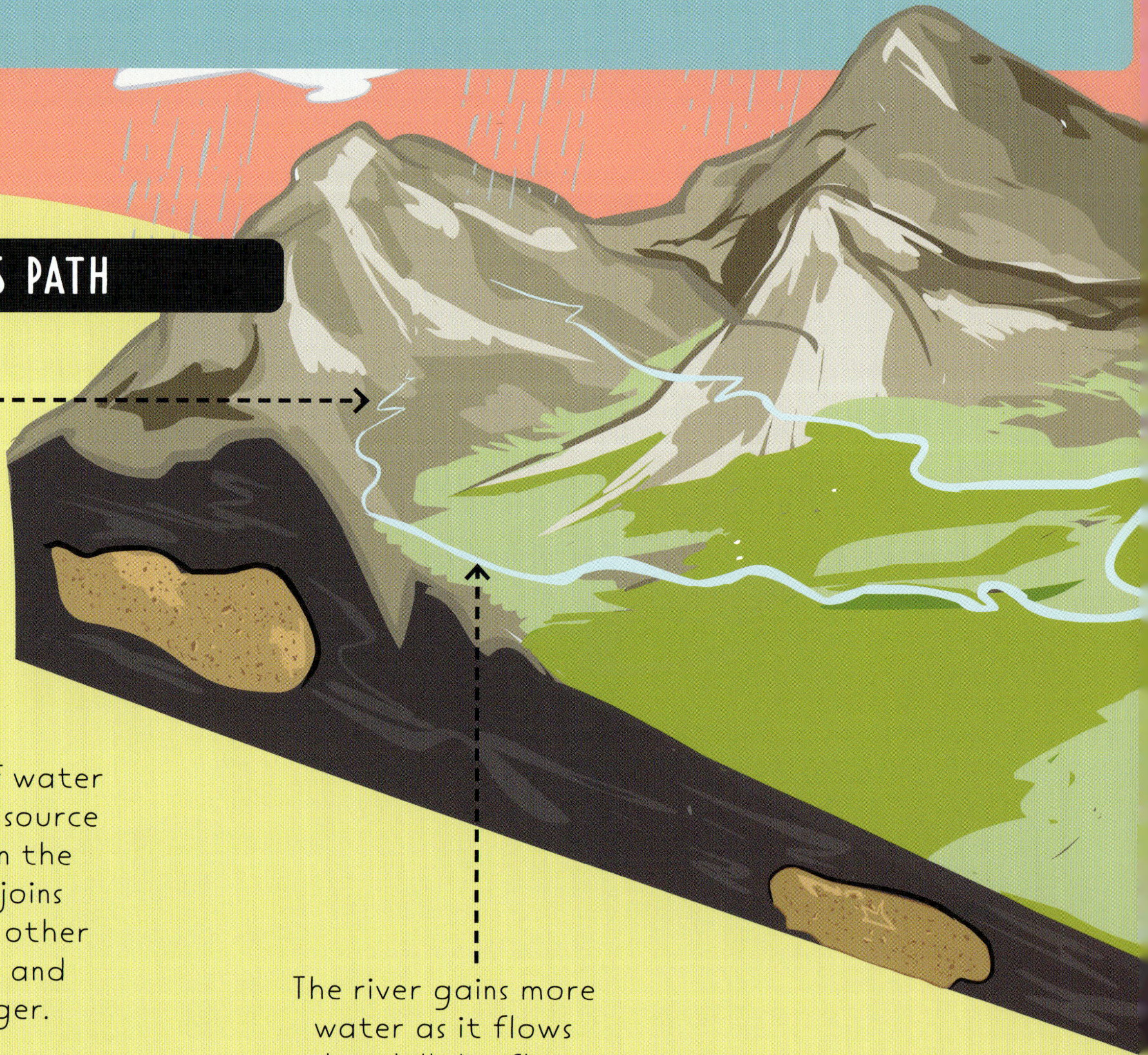

A tiny trickle of water flows from the source and runs down the mountain. It joins together with other small streams and becomes larger.

The river gains more water as it flows downhill. Its flow becomes bigger.

GET OUT THERE!

TRACK A RIVER

Do you live near a stream or river? Take a walk with an adult to see it, and then research it back at home. Where is its source? Where is its mouth?

QUIZ-TASTIC!

WHAT IS THE LONGEST RIVER IN AFRICA?

a) Congo River b) Zambezi River c) Nile River

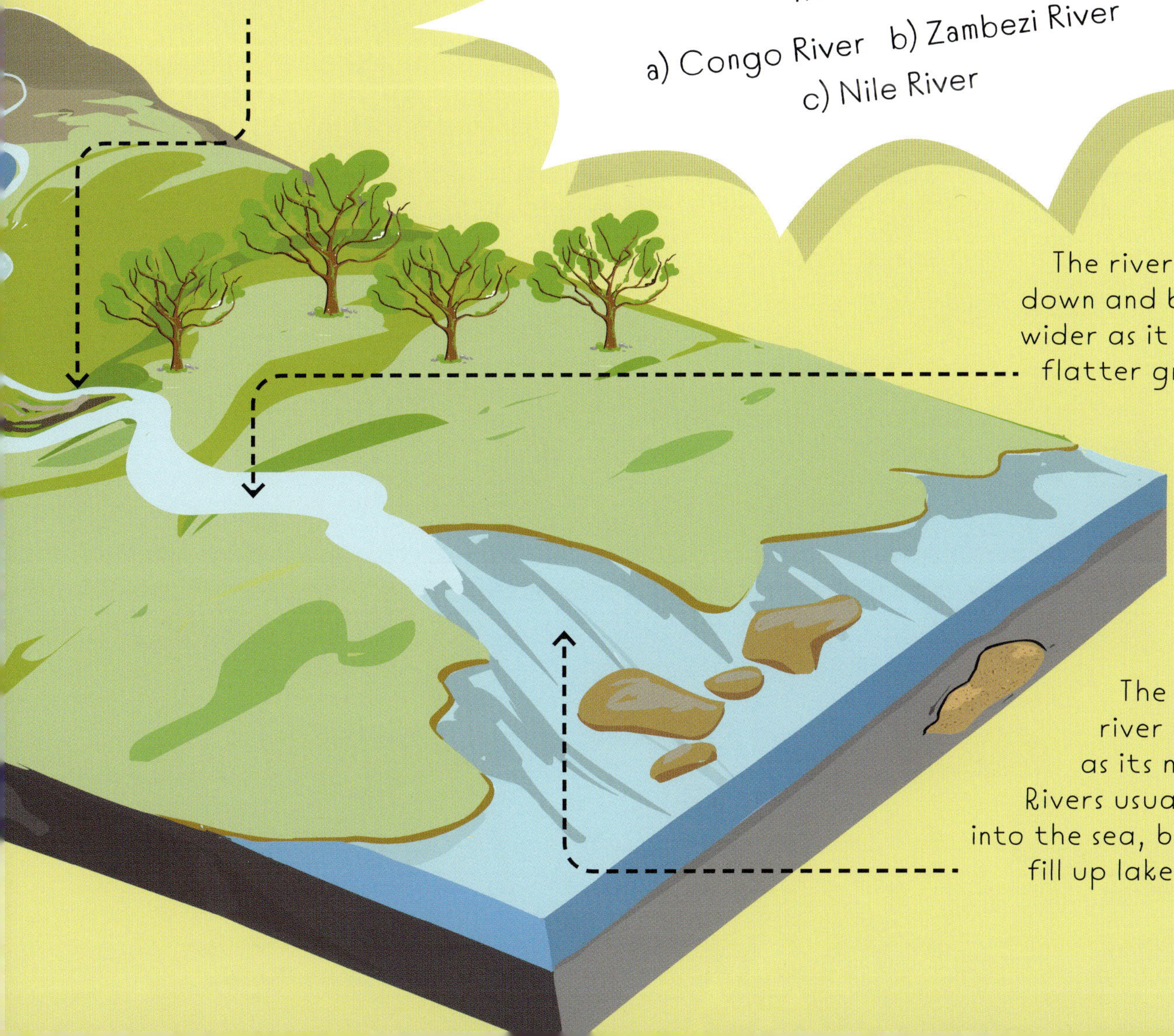

LAKES

A lake is surrounded by land.

WHAT MAKES A LAKE?

A lake is a large area of fresh water with land most or all of the way around it. It is deeper and larger than a pond. Sunlight can reach the bottom of a pond, but not the bottom of a lake. Lakes can be open or closed. Open lakes are connected to at least one river, while closed lakes aren't. The only way water can leave a closed lake is through evaporation.

NATURAL LAKES

Some lakes form naturally when a low area of land, known as a **basin**, fills with water. They can also form when a river floods because of extreme weather or as the result of a natural **dam** caused by a **landslide** or a fallen tree (or built by a sneaky beaver!).

I WONDER WOW!

Lake Baikal in Russia is the oldest and deepest lake on Earth. It is also the largest freshwater lake by volume. It has more than one-fifth of all fresh water on Earth's surface in it!

I MADE IT MYSELF!

Humans can also make lakes (often known as reservoirs). These lakes are made by deliberately damming a river or by digging out an **artificial** basin. Human-made lakes are built to provide a water supply for nearby towns or farms, generate **hydroelectric power,** or to control flooding.

OUTDOOR OBSERVATIONS

You might not live near a lake, but many parks and gardens have ponds. Can you find one in your area? What color is the water? What sort of wildlife lives in and around it?

OCEANS AND SEAS

Almost all of the water on Earth is found in the oceans and seas.

THE WORLD'S OCEANS

All of Earth's oceans are connected and form one huge body of salt water. But to make things easier, we divide it up into five oceans, and many smaller seas. The Pacific Ocean is the largest of the oceans. It covers about one-third of Earth's surface!

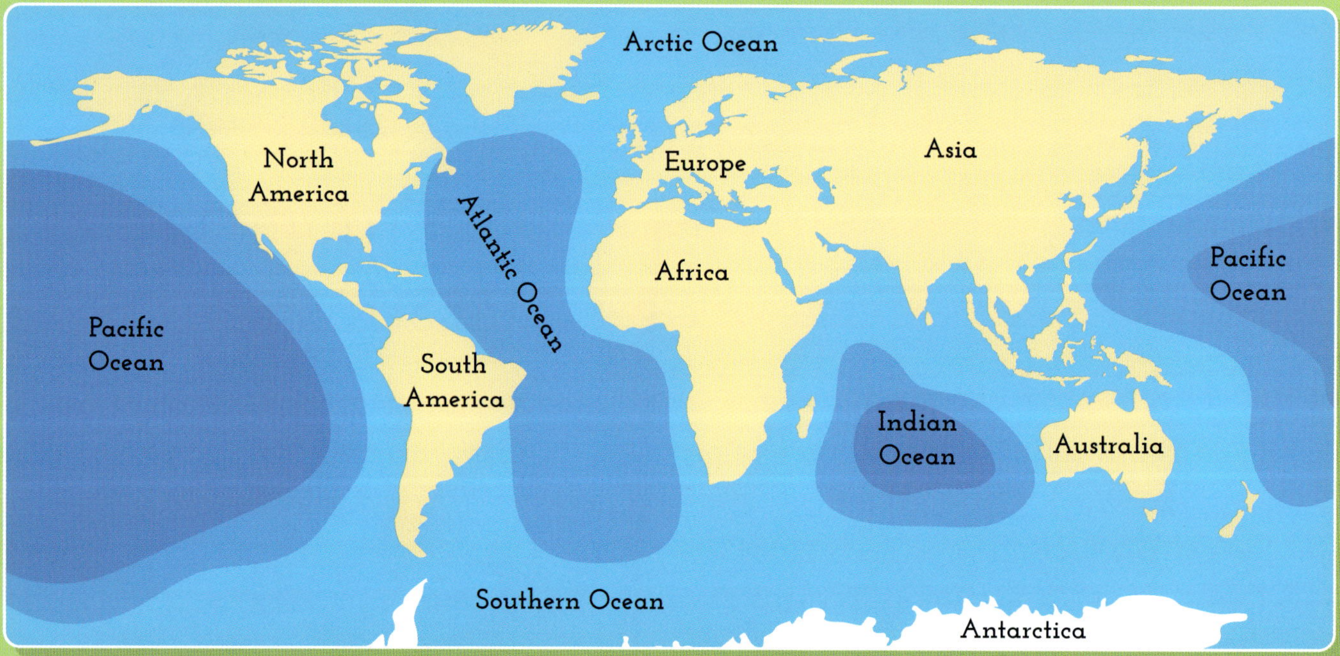

ON THE GO

Currents caused by wind and **water density** move seawater around the world's oceans and seas. The wind also creates waves on the surface of the water. The pull of **gravity** from the moon and the sun makes the sea level rise and fall. These movements are known as tides. They usually happen once or twice a day.

WATER MEETS LAND

The area where land meets the ocean is known as the coast. You can spot many different features along the coast.

GET OUT THERE!

COAST CHECK

If you live near the coast, ask an adult if you can visit it! Can you spot some of the different coastal features above, such as a pebble beach or a cliff?

I WONDER WOW!

The sea is salty because it contains mineral salts from soil that have been washed into the water.

WEIRD WATER

The movement of water can create some amazing features!

WOW, A WATERFALL!

When water flows over the ground, it erodes the rock. Some soft types of rock are worn away more quickly than harder rocks. This can create dramatic waterfalls.

1 A river flows over hard and soft rock.

2 The soft rock is worn away more quickly than the hard rock.

3 Water falls over the cliff created by the hard rock and a waterfall is born!

OUTDOOR OBSERVATIONS

Can you spot erosion in action in any rivers, lakes, or coastlines near your home? It could be something massive like a crumbling cliff or something small, like the slowly eroding banks of a stream.

QUIZ-TASTIC!

WHAT IS THE TALLEST WATERFALL IN THE WORLD?

a) Angel Falls, Venezuela

b) Niagara Falls, Canada and U.S.

c) Victoria Falls, Zambia and Zimbabwe

CURVE TO LAKE

Rivers often have curves, or meanders. Sometimes, the water in the river starts to form a shortcut between the curves, rather than going all the way around. This forms a new path for the river. The curve is eventually cut off from the rest of the river, creating a new lake. This type of lake is known as an oxbow lake.

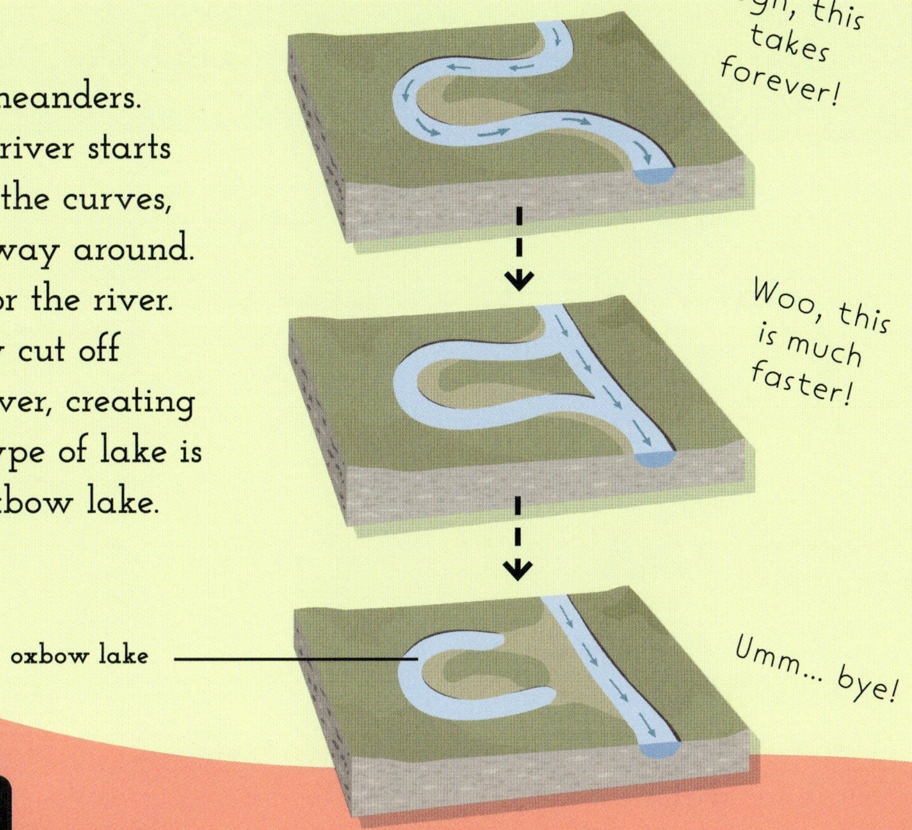

CLIFF CHANGES

Waves erode rock along the coast. This creates caves, arches, and other features.

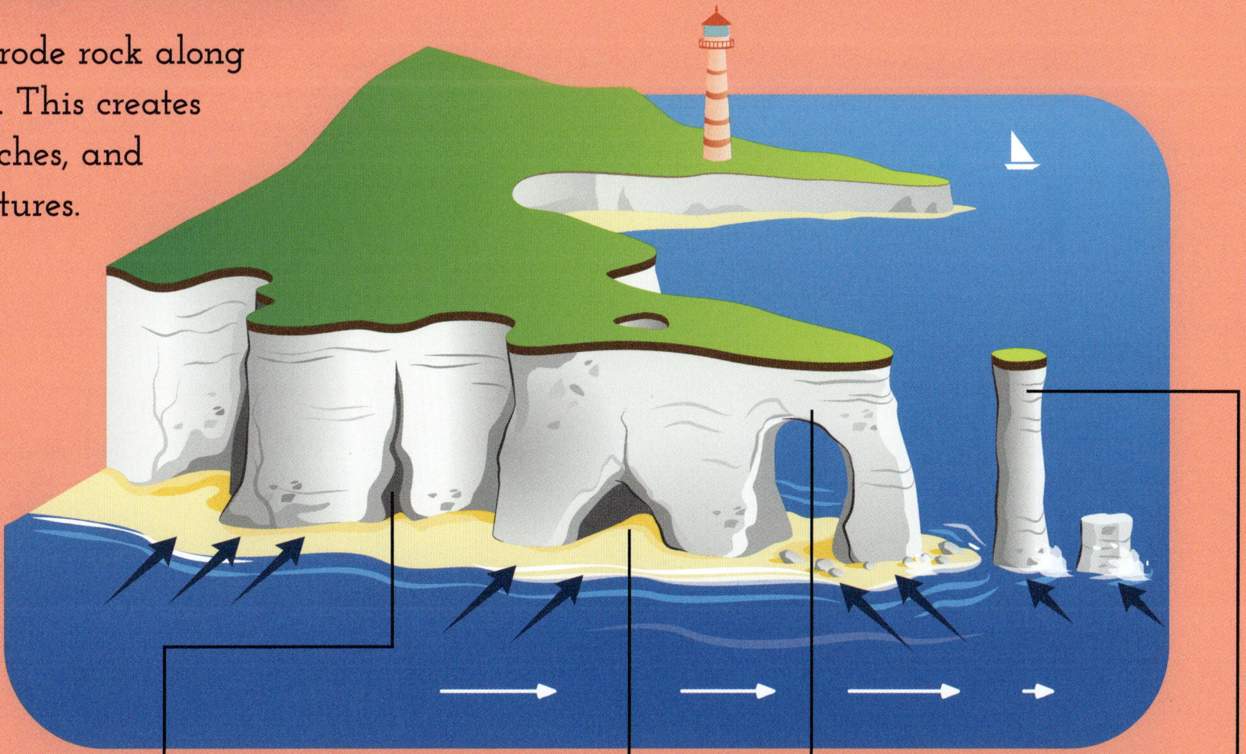

EVEN MORE WATER

Fresh water is found in many places ... not just lakes and rivers!

MORE THAN RIVERS

What comes to mind when you think of fresh water? Lakes, rivers and streams, right? But these bodies of water make up less than two percent of all the fresh water on Earth!

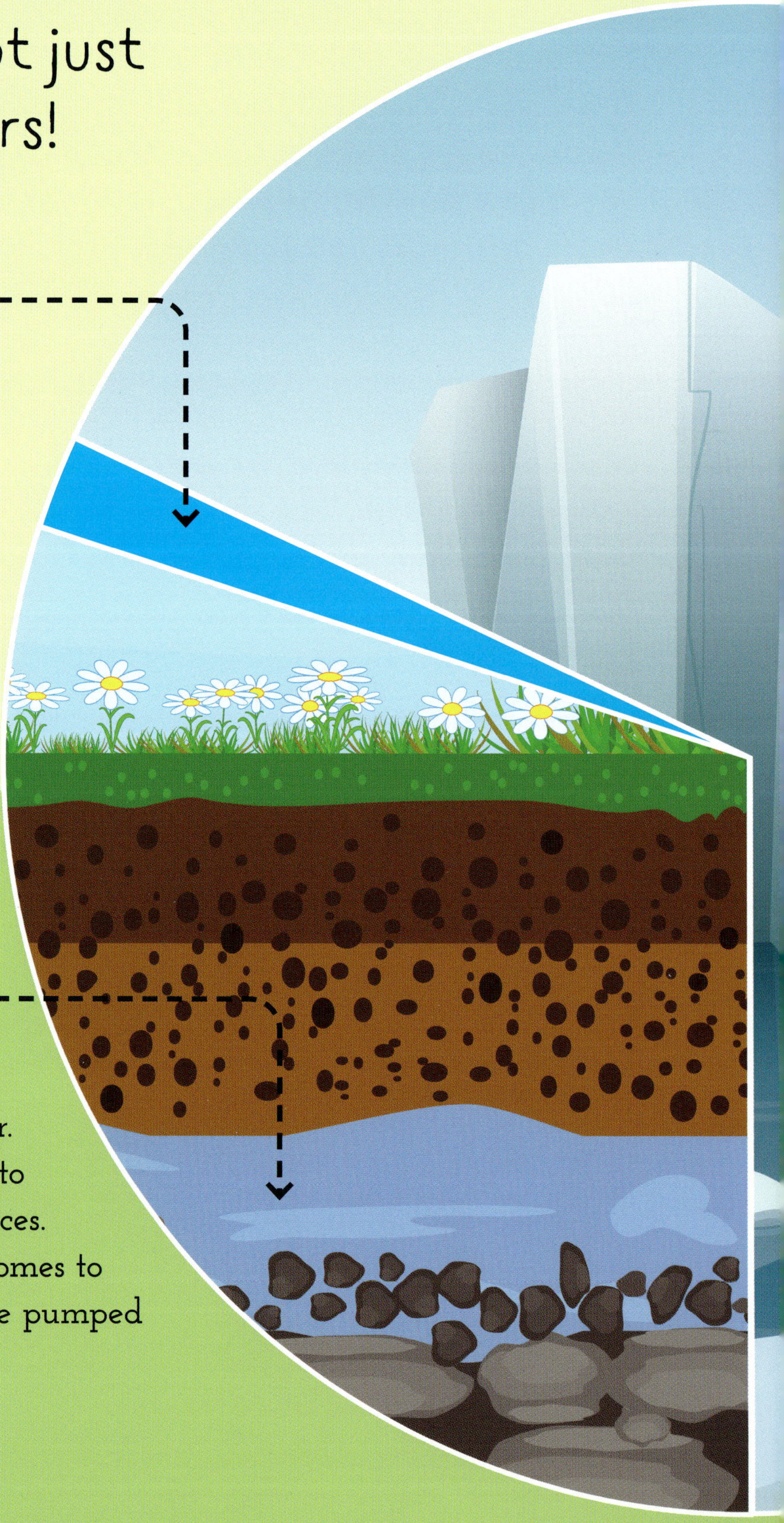

GOING UNDERGROUND

One-third of fresh water on Earth is hidden underground as groundwater. This is rainwater that has soaked into the soil and filled up cracks and spaces. Groundwater sometimes naturally comes to the surface as a spring. It can also be pumped out of the ground using a well.

NICE AND ICY

Massive ice caps and glaciers (moving sheets of ice) are found at the poles and on top of high mountains. They contain nearly 70 percent of all fresh water on Earth. **Global warming** is causing this ice to melt. This is destroying polar ecosystems and making sea levels rise around the world.

QUIZ-TASTIC!

WHERE IS THE LARGEST SHEET OF ICE ON EARTH?

a) Nepal b) Antarctica c) Greenland

GET OUT THERE!

RAIN TO GROUNDWATER

Rainwater soaks into the ground and becomes groundwater. Compare some different surfaces after it rains, such as a road, a grassy area, and a dirt path. Which surfaces absorb water quickly? Where does the water stay on the surface as puddles?

LIFE UNDERWATER

Aquatic animals and plants have adapted to life in the water.

BREATHING BASICS

Some aquatic animals, such as fish, can breathe underwater. They take in oxygen from the water using their **gills**. Most mammals, reptiles, and **amphibians** that live in the water don't have gills. They need to come to the surface to breathe air.

I WONDER WOW!

The Cuvier's beaked whale regularly holds its breath for an hour while looking for food underwater!

SWIMMING SMOOTHLY

Many aquatic animals swim with fins and flippers. They use these to push themselves through the water and to steer from side to side. Animals that live in water usually have smooth, **streamlined** bodies, which allow them to move easily through the water.

ROOTS? WHERE?

Aquatic plants are quite different from plants that live on land. One of the main differences is their roots ... well, their lack of roots! Most land plants use roots to hold the plant in place and take in **nutrients** and water. Many aquatic plants, on the other hand, don't have roots. If they do, it's just to hold the plant in place. They take in nutrients and water through their stem and leaves.

Some water plants have leaves that float on the surface, like these water lilies. Others live entirely underwater.

OUTDOOR OBSERVATIONS

Moving through the air is quite similar to moving through the water. Take a look at a bird flying. How does its movement and body compare to that of a fish?

WATERY WEBS

There are food webs in freshwater and saltwater ecosystems.

WHO EATS WHOM?

All of the animals in an ecosystem depend on plants or each other for food. For example, an otter eats fish like carp, which in turn eat aquatic plants. We can draw these connections in a diagram called a food web.

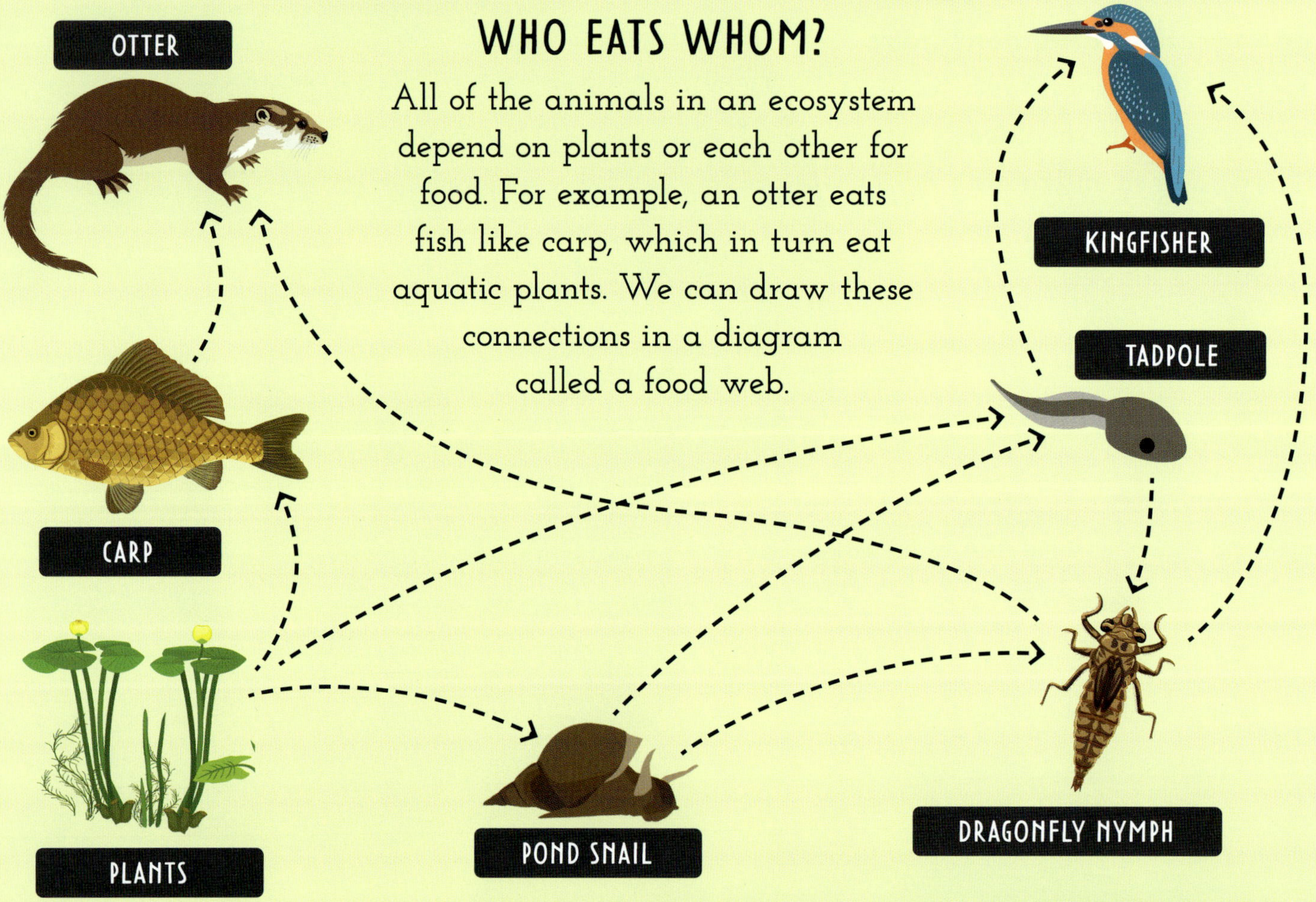

WHERE IN THE WEB?

Herbivores are at the bottom of food webs, just above plants. **Omnivores** and small **carnivores** are higher up the food web. Large carnivores are found at the top.

Large carnivores with no natural **predators** are called apex predators. In the ocean, killer whales and some sharks are apex predators.

The clue is in the name!

CONNECTED WEB

All of the living things in an ecosystem are connected. This means that if the **population** of one **species** goes down because of a problem, the other species that live there are affected too. Animals that eat that species would go hungry. Animals eaten by that species may, by contrast, increase in population.

QUIZ-TASTIC!

WHICH OF THESE OCEAN ANIMALS IS A HERBIVORE?

a) green turtle b) octopus
c) hammerhead shark

GET OUT THERE!

OBSERVE A FOOD WEB

We can see water food webs without going into the water. Spot an animal that lives near or in water. Using a guidebook or the internet, find out what that animal eats and which other animals eat it, and draw a food web.

THE WATER CYCLE

The water on Earth is constantly moving.

UP AND DOWN

The movement of water from Earth's surface to the atmosphere and back again is known as the water cycle. Water changes state as it moves through the water cycle.

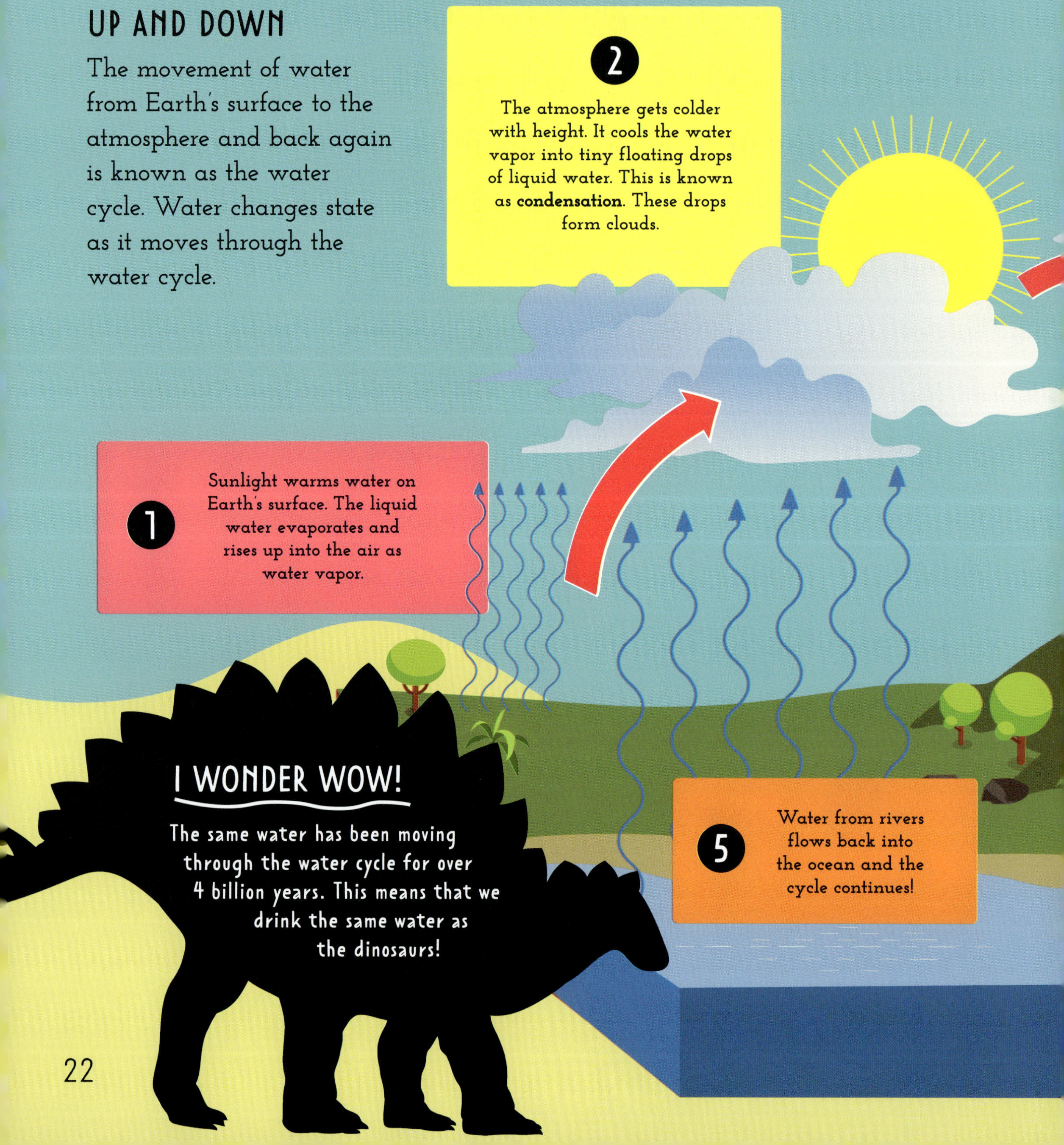

I WONDER WOW!

The same water has been moving through the water cycle for over 4 billion years. This means that we drink the same water as the dinosaurs!

3

The droplets get bigger and heavier. Eventually the water falls down to Earth as rain, or snow, hail, or sleet if the air temperature is low enough.

OUTDOOR OBSERVATIONS

How many different parts of the water cycle can you spot outside? Look at the picture on these pages for ideas.

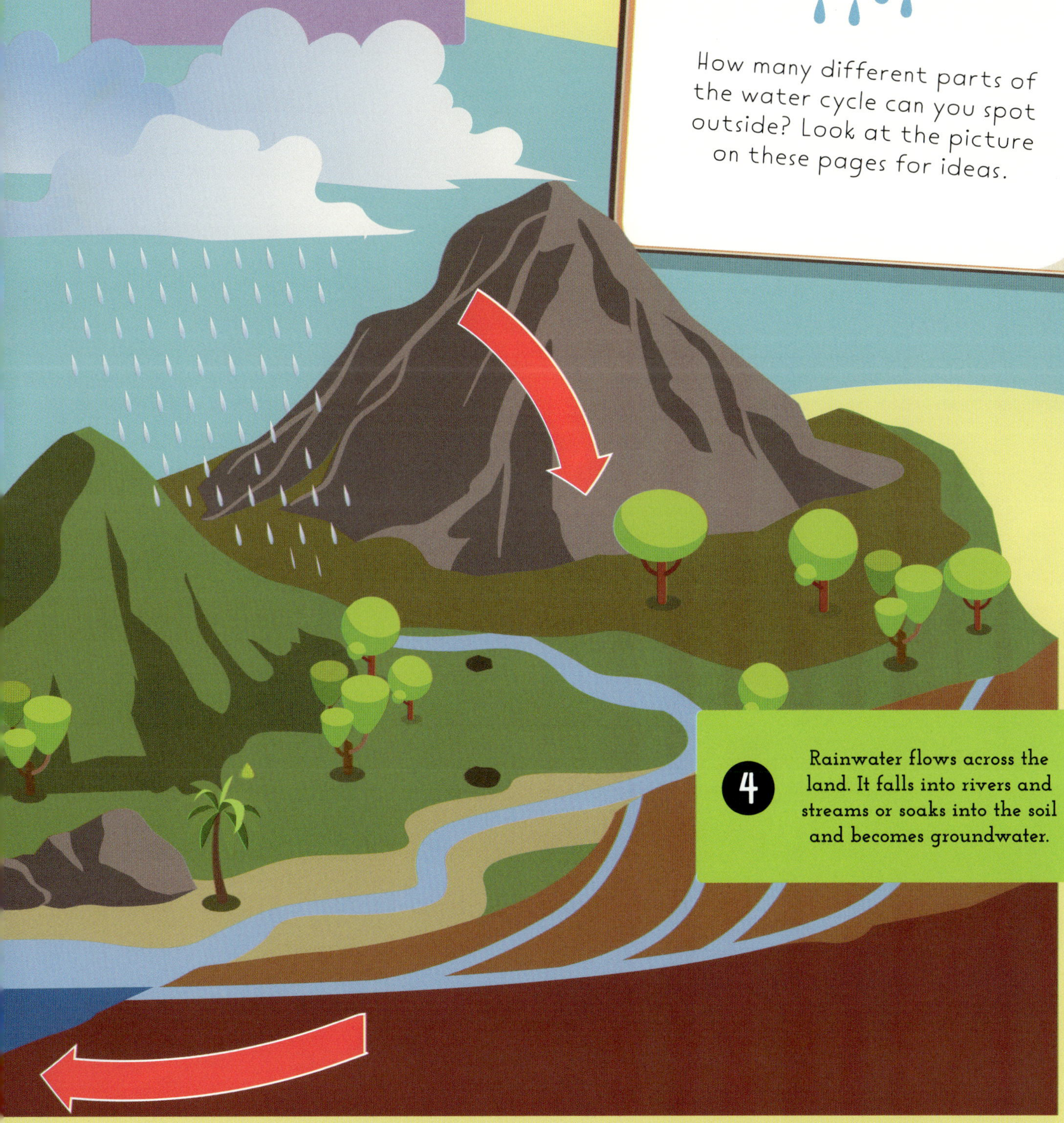

4

Rainwater flows across the land. It falls into rivers and streams or soaks into the soil and becomes groundwater.

PLASTIC PROBLEMS

Plastic pollution is a massive threat to water habitats.

LAND TO SEA

Most of the plastic pollution in the ocean comes from the land. It is dumped into the water, or is blown by the wind into the water. Once in the ocean, the wind, sunlight, and movement of the waves breaks down plastic into tiny pieces called microplastics.

When ocean animals eat microplastics, the plastics pass through the food web. They can end up in the fish and shellfish that we eat.

I WONDER WOW!

A garbage truck's worth of plastic ends up in our oceans every minute.

A DANGEROUS DINNER

Millions of aquatic animals are killed by plastic every year. Some mistake the plastic for food and eat it. The plastic damages their digestive system. Animals can also get trapped in plastic objects and packaging and drown.

GET OUT THERE!

TRASH CLEANUP

Picking up plastic waste on land will stop it from entering the water. Organize a cleanup with an adult. Wear gloves and use a trash picker. Don't touch anything sharp or dangerous.

STOP IT!

Reducing our use of plastic is the best way of preventing more plastic pollution. We also need to stop the plastic we do use from entering the ocean in the first place! Countries need to work together to find better ways to dispose of waste. Engineers have developed machines that can collect large pieces of rubbish from the ocean, but tiny microplastics are almost impossible to remove.

Here are some ways to reduce your plastic use:

Take a reusable shopping bag to the supermarket.

Carry a refillable water bottle.

Choose items with plastic-free packaging when possible.

WATER AT RISK

Plastic pollution isn't the only danger facing the water on Earth.

BIG PROBLEMS

Other forms of pollution and **climate change** are also massive threats to the fresh and salt water on Earth. They are damaging water ecosystems and threatening the clean, accessible water that people, plants, and animals need to survive.

DIRTY WATER

Rivers and lakes are polluted by **pesticides** from farming, chemicals from factories, and human waste from places with poor **sanitation**. This pollution harms the plants and animals that live in the water. If people drink or use the polluted water, it can make them very sick or even kill them.

Climate change caused by global warming is having a major impact on water around the world.

CAUSE

High temperatures are making lakes and rivers dry up.

Much less rain is falling in some areas.

EFFECT

People don't have enough water to use at home or to water crops.

Animals and plants don't have enough water to survive.

Other areas are experiencing much more rain than usual.

Floods become more common.

Polar ice is melting because of higher temperatures.

Sea levels are rising along the coasts.

Polar ecosystems are being destroyed.

The oceans are becoming less salty because more fresh water is being added to them. This affects the plants and animals that live there.

GET OUT THERE!

CHALLENGE YOUR LOCAL POLITICIAN

Write an email to your representatives in Congress and ask them what they are doing to reduce water pollution in your area and across the country. If they aren't doing anything, ask them to take action!

I WONDER WOW!

Just over 30 percent of schools around the world don't have access to clean water.

AWESOME ACTIVITIES

Try out these water projects!
Check with an adult before you begin.

BUILD A DAM

Make a dam in a shallow plastic tray. Gather natural materials such as sticks, stones, mud, or leaves. Use the materials to build a dam in the center of the tray. Then, pour water into one side. Does the dam block the water? If not, how could you improve it?

VANISHING ARTWORK

Get creative and see evaporation in action by creating a vanishing artwork. Paint with water on a paved surface or wall on a hot day. Watch as the water evaporates and your artwork disappears in front of your eyes!

MAKE YOUR OWN RAINCATCHER

Save rainwater and use it to water your plants on dry days. Wash and dry a large plastic bottle with a handle and a lid. Ask an adult to cut off the base of the bottle. Screw the lid on and turn the bottle over so that the lid is pointing down.

Tie it with string to a fence or an outdoor pole. You may need to wrap the string around the bottle's handle for support. Once your raincatcher is full, unscrew the lid and fill up your watering can!

WATER XYLOPHONE

Did you know that you can make music with water? All you need are at least four glasses that are around the same size, water, and a spoon.

Fill each glass with a different amount of water and tap gently to make a sound. Organize them from least to most water, and you've made your own water xylophone!

GLOSSARY

amphibian – an animal that lays eggs in water, but can live on land or in water

aquatic – describes something that lives in, grows in or is connected to water

artificial – made by people

atmosphere – the mixture of gases, including water vapor, that surrounds Earth

basin – a dip in the ground often shaped like a bowl where water can collect

carnivore – an animal that only eats other animals

climate change – change in Earth's weather patterns, often as a result of human activity such as burning coal, oil, and gas to create electricity or other types of energy

condensation – to change from a gas into a liquid

current – the movement of water in one direction

dam – a wall built across a river that stops the river's flow

ecosystem – all the living things in an area, as well as the nonliving parts such as soil and rocks

erode – to wear away

estuary – the area at the mouth of a river where fresh water mixes with salt water

evaporate - to change from a liquid into a gas

gas – something, such as air, that can expand and float out of an open container

gills – the organs through which fish and some other aquatic animals breathe

global warming – an increase in world temperatures

gravity – a force that pulls objects together

herbivore – an animal that only eats plants

hydroelectric power – power generated by moving water

ice cap – a thick layer of ice that covers the land

landslide – when rock and earth quickly fall down a slope

liquid – something, such as milk, that flows

nutrient – something that plants or animals need to grow and be healthy

omnivore – an animal that eats plants and other animals

pesticide – a chemical sometimes used by farmers to kill unwanted animals that eat their crops

population – the number of one type of living thing in a certain area

predator – an animal that kills and eats other animals

sanitation – taking dirty water and waste away from buildings to help keep living areas clean and safe for humans

solid – something, such as a piece of wood, that holds its shape

species – a type of living thing

streamlined – with a smooth shape that makes it easier to move through air or water

turbine – a machine that turns moving liquid or gas into power

water density - how much space water takes up

water vapor - water in the form of a gas

FURTHER READING

BOOKS

Dicker, Katie. *Clean and Safe Water*. New York, NY: PowerKids Press, 2023.

Gieseke, Tyler. *The Water Cycle*. Minneapolis, MN: Pop!, 2023.

Lundgren, Julie K. *Water, Water Everywhere*. New York, NY: Crabtree Publishing Company, 2022.

WEBSITES

kids.britannica.com/kids/article/ocean/346185
Find out more about the oceans.

www.bbc.co.uk/bitesize/topics/z6p6qp3/articles/z3wpp39
Learn more about the water cycle and check your knowledge with a quiz.

climatekids.nasa.gov/10-things-water/
Discover 10 amazing facts about water.

QUIZ-TASTIC ANSWERS

Page 7 c, Page 9 c, Page 14 a, Page 17 b, Page 21 a

INDEX